We are Catholic

written by Christine Way Skinner
illustrations by Céleste Gagnon

Nihil Obstat: Rev. Ivan Camilleri, V.G.
                    Archdiocese of Toronto

Imprimatur: Thomas Cardinal Collins
                    Archbishop of Toronto

                    20 March 2015

Twenty-Third Publications
1 Montauk Avenue
Suite 200
New London, CT 06320
(860) 437-3012
(800) 321-0411
www.23rdpublications.com

ISBN: 978-1-62785-096-4

Printed in Canada.

For my children and my husband,
Michael, whom I love with all my heart.
~ CWS

To my husband Andrew and my children
Amélie and Elliott for their constant
support and love.
~ CG

This book belongs to:

_____

My parish: _____

The school I attend: _____

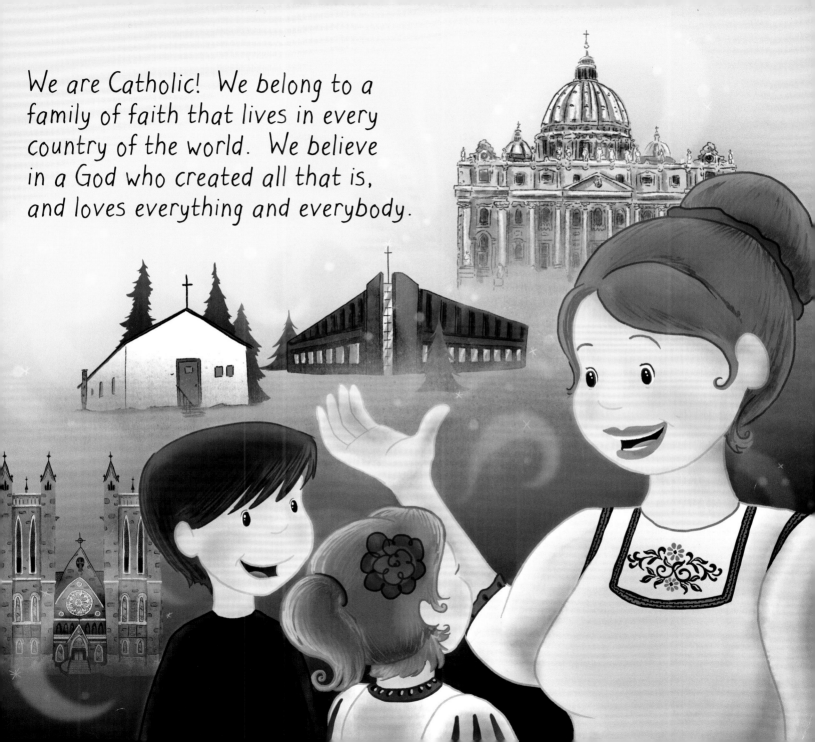

We are Catholic! We belong to a family of faith that lives in every country of the world. We believe in a God who created all that is, and loves everything and everybody.

We believe that God is Father, Son and Holy Spirit. Jesus, God's son, came to live among us and to teach us about His Father's love. He is still with us in a special way.

We celebrate our faith in church, at school and at home. We celebrate Sunday — the day of the Lord!

The priest and the parish ministers welcome us at the doors of the church.

We make the Sign of the Cross with holy water.

We sing songs

and say prayers.

We listen to God's holy Word from the Bible.

We use bread and wine to remember Jesus' special offering of Himself with his friends.

We celebrate wonderful feasts all year long.

We light candles on the Advent
wreath to get ready for Christmas.

We celebrate Jesus' birth at Christmas...
and the visit of the Wise Men at Epiphany.

We have our foreheads marked with ashes on Ash Wednesday.

We pray and fast and give to the poor during Lent.

We wave palms on Palm Sunday.

We ring bells and light candles at Easter.

We rejoice at Pentecost.

We celebrate important times in our lives.

We also celebrate
our faith at home.

We have statues
and holy pictures
on our walls.

We say grace before we eat and share our bread with the hungry.

We say prayers when we get up in the morning

...and before we go to bed.

What a wonderful gift it is to belong to the Catholic family.

Dear Parents and Caregivers:

Here are some ideas to nurture your child's Catholic faith.

● **Keep the Sabbath** ~ The most important way to develop your child's Catholic identity is to celebrate Eucharist weekly and make Sundays special.

● **Celebrate the Liturgical Year** ~ The liturgical year provides the rituals and routines that children need and love.
- Celebrate the church's two major seasons: Advent/Christmas and Lent/Easter.
- Use a liturgical calendar.
- Prepare for Christmas using an Advent wreath or religious Advent calendar.
- Set up a manger scene.
- Leave your tree up until the Feast of the Epiphany on January 6th.
- Receive ashes on Ash Wednesday.
- Give, fast and pray during Lent.
- Attend Holy Week liturgies.
- Feast at Easter and Pentecost.
- Honour saints' days.

● **Participate in Parish Life** ~ Help children develop a sense of belonging to their parish by greeting the pastor and other ministers after Mass, getting to know other parishioners and attending parish events.

● **Engage the Senses** ~ Catholic sacramental life involves all five senses.

Sight
- Make faith visible in your home with crosses, pictures of patron saints and guardian angels and blessed palms.
- Arrange a bedroom prayer corner with baptismal candles and religious images.
- Give children holy cards.

Taste
Make meals events of thanksgiving and joyful communion so that our children learn to understand the importance of Eucharist more completely.

Eat special foods on feast days, fast from meat on Fridays, make Lenten pretzels and Easter bread and serve dessert on Sundays.

Hearing

Read religious stories.
Sing Bible songs.
Have times of silence during Lent.
Ring bells and sing Alleluias during the Easter season.

Smell

Our sense of smell fosters enduring memories, feelings and associations.
Cook particular foods for important feasts.
Light scented candles or incense for prayer.
Use real lilies for Easter and evergreen for Advent wreaths and Christmas trees.

Touch

Embody and communicate God's love to your children though loving touch.
Trace a cross on your children's foreheads before bed.
Pray the rosary.

Foster Prayer ~ It is vital to build prayer into family life. On pages 30 and 31, you'll find two traditional prayers to pray together.
Say grace before meals.
Bless children (with or without holy water) before they leave for school.
Say prayers in the morning and at bedtime.
Keep a prayer book, crucifix and Bible on the bedside table.
Read scripture stories before bed.
Teach children to listen to God during periods of short silent meditation.

By incorporating these rituals and rhythms of the church year into our family life, the entire family will grow in love for, and appreciation of, our wonderful heritage of community, prayer and celebration.

Our Father

Our Father, who art in heaven, hallowed be thy name;
thy kingdom come,
thy will be done on earth as it is in heaven.
Give us this day our daily bread,
and forgive us our trespasses,
as we forgive those who trespass against us;
and lead us not into temptation,
but deliver us from evil.
Amen.

Hail Mary

Hail Mary, full of grace, the Lord is with you;
blessed are you among women,
and blessed is the fruit of your womb, Jesus.
Holy Mary, mother of God,
pray for us sinners
now and at the hour of our death.
Amen.

Christine Way Skinner has been a parish catechist for 24 years. She has a Master of Divinity from Harvard Divinity School and is the author of *Jesus Invites Me to the Feast: My First Eucharist Journal* (Liguori). When she is not trying to find inclusive, compelling and creative ways to pass on the Catholic Church's tradition, Christine enjoys reading, art, gardening and trying to convince her husband, Michael, and their house full of children that they really do love playing board games with her.

Céleste Gagnon is a full-time illustrator and designer. Over the last 15 years, Céleste has worked on many projects, including books, magazines, novel covers, merchandise, clothing, and fabric design. She loves what she does and the variety of work that comes with being an illustrator. When she is not working, Céleste likes reading, hiking and enjoying nature with her husband and their two young children.